"I didn't grow up in Kansas, but while reading Rob Yates' *Son of God* I got singed by the prairie fire realism of his plain-spoken verse, transported to a place where he was born in 1982 'in a part of Kansas that stayed in 1958' in poems where 'pain is a time machine.' He confronts the oppression of growing up in a religious world his verse attempts to escape, but instead he has drinks with these demons and looks to guiding future generations toward independence from the dogmas of the past. These poems are new generation prayers and meditations that expose truths with humor and hard-fought wisdom in a collection that will resonate with many."

–Kevin Ridgeway, author of *Too Young to Know* (Stubborn Mule Press) and *Invasion of the Shadow People* (Luchador Press)

Son of God

Poems by Rob Yates

Spartan
Press

Spartan Press

Kansas City, Missouri

spartanpress.com

Spartan
Press

Acknowledgments

The author would like to thank the editors of the following publications, where some of these poems first appreared:

Mikrokosmos – Haunted, Byzantine
Rejection Lit – Worked
Riot Mag – Moonlit Path

Table of Contents:

II

Don't try.

-"Hank" Bukowski

For Jennifer, Autumn, Jocelyn, Aurora and Yoshi too.

For Danny and Meredith, my friends and supporters during my residency at Wichita State's MFA program.

Thank you for all that you are.

I

Prairie Fire

I was born in 1982, in part
of Kansas that stayed in 1958;
ashtrays line every desk and
it is still "quite a thing to marry
a black" -one of the nicer things
I hear my aunt or cousins called,
or hurled at men on street corners.
Bullying built character
and streetlamps, lighting disdain
thicker than the smoke
in each building. Tar stench spills
into the guts of uncles on
an unemployment line, meat
processors with yellowing
beards and idle fingers. The
warehouse brick ovens belch fire,
processing fewer pay stubs, stoking
the meat-grinder to churn out
alcoholism and social friction.
Factory workers are squeezed and bled
like a Christmas orange or the throat
of a lover that takes their rage.
Store fronts domino against one another
down main street. We chalk the sidewalks
with smiles. My grandfather,
a watchmaker, is forced to trade in
his Swiss tools for a semi-truck,
arthritis for a broken back.

He splits Wrigley's gum in half
to spare enough mint
for every grandchild.
Lighting the hearth of crumbling lives,
we end each year wishing
on a Mall Santa's lap.

Roosevelt Elementary Lunchroom

The table closest to the kitchen was by reservation only:
a destination for split-lips and detention slips

            I sit alone

Thirty minutes for
dining on stares of children
drinking all their milk, for
surveying wounds and muttered cursing:
Fuck peas.
Fuck sixth graders.
Fuck me.

A lunch lady sits
with me after a week or two,
tiny tip-toe-heel visit breaking
up solitary, confined monotony.
Her mid-century dress, pressed neat
below pin-curls gone ten years gray.
Her eyes match mine, speckled
blue as the robin-egg plate
where I push around cold potatoes,
shaping them into the dunes of some far-off planet.
Slender fingers hold out an apple,
"Eat, you must eat." Those blue's
study mine with glassy worry
at each small bite.
I may have been a "bad kid,"
       alright,

but I was still her grandchild.

Meatbag

Maintain a body
Endure all of its pokes,
    jabs,
drilled teeth.

Vomit, strep throat
braces, bullying
and straightening you
up for work.
Produce.
Propagate.

Once you can feed yourself,
add more mouths.
Fill them with little prayers
and have them bite down on
"It will be better tomorrow."

Food stamps address this week,
maybe the next.
Live another day, hallelujah,
breaking down straightened teeth
on boot leather chicken.

Frost coats this room of black.
There are no windows, no
stars to wish on,
but cross your heart,
"You'll have sugar plums
when you sleep."

Runaway I

First attempt. Second grade.
The suitcase with a teddy bear on the cover packed
with a pillow and favorite blanket.
Easing out the back door so it won't creak.
Back yard, a shroud.
I realize I don't know
anything.
where to go
what to do
how to get to grandma's house-
My breath clouds toward a half-moon.

Something from the ally skitters
and my feet match pace back inside
to cry
under an unpacked blanket.

In the morning, my parents tell me
they watched my escape from a window.
watched my deliberation.
watched my confusion.

And had a good laugh.

I stole two books from school
The Crucible and *Howl*

I walked out, each tucked in a lunchbox
under plastic wrapped and half-eaten bologna
weighted down by an apple.
I rehearsed being caught in the mirror,
mumbling excuses over a Batman toothbrush.
Learning to lie. I wait for librarian police
to toss my mattress and throw me in a slammer.
No one knows.

I read Ginsberg under flannel with a flashlight,
the ones made of burnt orange plastic -
a boy's first lightsaber, D-cell batteries taken from a radio.
I hid Arthur and Allen between CD's labeled
EXPLICIT CONTENT
in a space between the dresser drawers.
- a good place to store a bottle of hooch
or a little weed,
but I was a good church kid.
Knowledge was my contraband at home.

Both are still on my shelf, allegedly.
Yellowed by time and smudges of peanut butter
on pages 12 and 13, little drops of tea and whiskey
by 23.

Waxing '96

Turtle wax. The scent of sixty-six years of Ford being massaged with a yellow-sponge-starship included in the cap. I scoop heaps of the key lime and work it into the hood of my Falcon Coupe. My sixteen-year-old hands tremble after hours of turning the coarse, chalk-like surface into a mirror of pearl. My face is dark in the reflection. Tan and summer sweat. Blond hair in the breeze. I am Mad Max. I am Han Solo. I am young enough to whisper these things to myself.

The hood is smooth and warm under my legs. Hands cracked dry. The green paste caked over my flesh is preserving it like a corpse. Six cylinders power the radio enough to catch every other word rattled over the creak of tree branches - arthritic fingers grabbing at a setting sun. Deep reds shift the atmosphere, welcomed by the dry crooning of John Mccrea. Dim-lights in my cabin flicker in the cicada-filled dark, and the engine whines. A witch's moon beckons me onward. Grounded.

Son, you're running away on a globe.

Dad always wanted to be a pastor

Genesis 22

God asked my father to take me
to the mountain and sacrifice
a life. Cost of paradise,
the blood owed - mine.

He gazed longingly at the heavens,
knife at my spine.
I am here Lord,
his voice an anxious whine.

Gripping the handle, begging,
sublime. *Bring down the knife.*
Father breathes heavy,
How many times?

Ninety Pound Wuss

I wrote "imitation is suicide" on a black notebook
     in white out ink.

tapped out in vein struggle
take a breath while eating curls
of seven dollar habit that takes it
Makes it
Quicker

I don't want to get old
I don't want the taste on my lips when I kiss death
     to be bitter.

Runaway II

Second attempt. Seventh grade.
Written on back of English Quiz and taped
    to a bedroom door.
Letter:

Dad-

If I could do anything to not be
like this
I would.

Teenage Tapedeck

Music is a live wire. At school, she hands it to me in a
    bottle, the mixtape changing hands, becoming current
        jumping
firing
    synapse

from the cassette to ear drums.

Two people in
    a cosmic moment
        strung together
    by cassette
tape.

Don't say I love you
Give me your song.

Maintenance Request

In the classroom
the ceiling tiles sag,
and when it rains
tiles on the floor canvas
mystery stains.
Desks shuffle
to escape the weight
of repetition,
repetition,
Perdition.

Neon bulbs baptize
but nobody can see
her eyes   but me.
Sunglasses inside,
that can't quite hide
contusion,
dark and diffusion
on the cheek
of the girl floating up, up
to find the spaces between the lights.
Expiring,
flickering and firing,

she burns out.

Runaway III

Third attempt. October, 1998.
My father says:

You can't leave.
I know for the first time that I can.

When he throws himself onto the hood of my car I shift
to reverse, flattening gas pedal to the floor. He
rolls off into the rearview mirror,
disappearing in dust and dark.

Time

You eat the leaves before they hit
the ground in single smacks of your
mouth. World eater. Taking the crispy
skin of each year with a smile.
The first frost blankets in a
a kiss, cold as the grave. Father
Christmas, give us another Spring
morning.

untitled effort

Date night 2014, my fiancé wants to paint together. She
is an artist and her parents are artists. The kind that say,
*selling a piece in Aspen or Santa Fe means adding a zero to the
price.*

Her fingers glide into the deep reds and pinks the way
a baker kneads dough. I have never touched a brush.
Taking time to comb through colors in the old cigar
boxes where she keeps her pigments, I make little pools
of favorites on a paper plate. Al Green tells us we'll be
together, more softly, with each popped cork. Sunset is
piercing the windows, reflecting off a building on the
Chicago skyline. Caught in mind, I set to work. Her
eyes hunched over my shoulder at the last stroke with
frowned silence.

After the divorce, I found it. My painting. Untitled
effort. Scratched and punctured canvas rotting beneath
a bed and pile of books. She shoved it there that night,
while I slept off the wine. There was never enough
room for her work - rotated across three bedrooms of
walls. There was never enough room for me.

West 80

I drove through Salt Lake twice, everything was closed.
Left for Albuquerque, mid-afternoon -
stoned, looking for water and a route to Roswell.
I penciled the last stop for gas
between Oakley and Kit Carson
in the margins of a half-finished novel.

Camping

We put tents up next to each other
so it would feel less cold with
someone so close.
So close that we share
a sleeping bag when
the fire goes down
and the night sky wraps us
in twinkling arms.
We dance and writhe under
stars and the blanket of night.

Dawn

Tending coffee over firewood.
silent in the mist of bird mornings.
Precious seconds of life

without sirens or fingerprints

you hold my hand

the one with the thumb and forefinger you break
while I bleed into the sink under mirror of black

and smile at me in the morning.

East 80

There are corners where
the Chicago fire still hides embers.
I wallow where the night air burns
going mad with the slapping of bay waves.

A pall rises as cabs slip into curbs;
drifters light what's left in an ashtray cooling
atop iron tables behind steel gates.
Still warm, a little life left, kindling.
Discarded, but put to use -
like you and me.

Byzantine

Our wounds did a waltz
in the cracking Colorado adobe,
where we broke glasses,
and boundaries crumbled
on the thin-varnished floor.

Blood contorted the ruddy trim
of our Kansas bungalow,
after your knuckles darted past
the perpetual mockery
battering my face to paste.

Neighbors scuttled the streets like rats,
coursing and feasting together
as streetlamps screamed go.
Inside, I tap at my first bruise
in the mirror where you glow.

Haunting the mist
of our first nights
where fog clutched at gravestones,
a captive audience gawking
at our kissing in the snow.

I ~~miss~~ hate you when my scars tingle,
especially when they start to show.

The Last Time I Saw my Grandfather I

It's Christmas at the small slabhouse
my father calls a farm:
three dogs
some deer
a barn owl
No harvest or grains. Father is a reaper of souls,
his toll: donations and attention via Sunday service.
My Grandpa sits on a couch in the mobile home glow-up,
recently relocated from a retirement community
to the edge of Kansas nowhere-
because it's better for ~~him~~ them.
My mother and father are circling in earshot
like buzzards scavenging carrion from a conversation.
Grandma has been gone a year and Grandpa is already
as dead inside as the winter grass.
He begs me to forgive my father,
with water running down his stubbled chin
as blood price.
Forgive them.
Family is all that matters.
Life is too short not to forgive.

I'll try. I say it.
I choke these two words through a thick throat,
strangling the truth, ready
to drown from my first teardrop.
I hug the old man, trying to squeeze his tears away like
wringing water from a rag.

Then I flee.

The Last Time I Saw my Grandfather II
It's not the time mother

She follows me to the car, grinding down
the gravel of the driveway with her flats.
What did your father ever do to you?
The wind is still today,
but what I say nearly blows her over-
who her husband is when she's not looking,
what she looks away from or says *is in the past,*
when she is asleep- how he peels off his mask and washes
it down the sink to become the monster in my closet.
She points a finger toward her ear, twirling it in a
    maddening circle.
It's 90's for, *you're retarded.*
She doesn't say *You're retarded.*
She says, *You better go get some more of that
ther-a-py,* drawing out each syllable, *Because you're...*
Her vitriol is running out of gas, radiating something
between hatred and panic.
With the E-light on, she revs up her engines to burn out
the driveway and last fuel to drive home ever again-
sharp and sudden her horn and headlights flare,
like warning a deer to run or end up a carcass.
She crashes head on, firing into the mumbling screeches
that she thinks a *retard* makes.

My grandfather died a month later-
heart dropped like a stone on my parent's floor.

Bloodline

A window hangs
open for Spring
air drifting through, I slip
screen in with the death flies.
No invitation. I am the silent scream.
I bite your neck,
drink deep. Invading the
thrashing nightmared
sleep. Puncturing skin and soul,
old wounds, small holes torn fresh red new-
Slake need, leaving you
                in the cold sweat blanket, vanish
-ing mist collecting in the corners
of wild eyed
terror.
You'll miss me,
bleed,
and write sad drunken thoughts
on a napkin left on the bedside table-
where your wife is framed, still smiling
back.
write sad,
write sad
memory and sleep atop
a thousand feathers, blood stained and
tickling monsters back into
your dreams.

Kindred
wake weary-
drink.

Borders

A line appears at my feet,
fury splinters the dirt
and tickles my throat
on spider legs
patrolling the distance
between us.
My passport falls down a gutter drain,
the mud and wet curling pages
and stamps that
dissolve into blurry colors,
riding drain-water
into the dark.
I consolidate my side of the room,
side of the bed
side of the office
side of my mind,
kicking small rocks across
the imaginary divide.
The schism growing wide,
and wider,
disfunction fed
and grown by time.

II

Poetry is chain smoking

Making mandala in ash with
smudged fingers. Collecting up what's
left in the bowl, scavenging for butts with a
drag or two left in them when the pack runs low.
Filtered love. Menthol flavored madness cooling the
    tongue.
Trying to quit. Coming back for the last time,
this time. Inhaling the existential until
it burns down, singeing the last moments of evening
    on fingertips.
Finger habits. A reason to get your coat and shoes.
    Aired out.
The scent of cheap motels and rental cars,
changing the taste of everything from morning oatmeal
to lover's lips. Held so lovingly when lit, then usually on
    its way
to the trash.

Lady from Brighton

Last week I met a lady online.
She has a Jesus bathroom.
It's one of those strange hobbies
that springs up in the wake of a divorce.
Each inch of white is plastered
with every kind of look that only Jesus
and five-dollar-decorating can muster.
Framing references of our Lord over
a porcelain throne.

I tell her about the dinosaur pop-up park I drove by
yesterday. Text pictures of a chomping maw
above arms that swing with mechanical imprecision.
Mouths agape, facing the sky like *Peanuts* characters
on a holiday special. We are both trying to get out
of the house and coming up with strange reasons to try.

I say it's fucking cold because I don't understand
Celsius. The icicles on my car door can articulate
what I can't calculate. She likes my bad poetry.
I learn to fall in love with cadence. Because it's far
too dangerous to meet.

fever pitch

We read poetry downtown where it's all wheatgrass and no liquor. I hesitate the pen over the sign-up page, cause honestly, I hate that shit. But she just keeps asking. She introduces herself to my friend and laughs too loud. Her hands are on my back because that's who she is. She snaps and bares teeth, tracing my tattoos - taking my picture and keeping me talking. When it's time to share my words, she presses herself into me and I lay back and try to enjoy it - otherwise, how am I ever going to get ahead in this biz?

Natural Disasters

Pompeii in flash of light,
a white-hot moment of disbelief-
clutched children and lovers
swept up in ash and confusion.
Burning out conscience
a civilization tumbles
and tumbles
down
in a wave of last breaths.

At Harry's bar
its all so loud;
I'm trying to soak up
the wet floors and bad decisions,
drinking in sight and sound
of people too rose-cheeked to see
past three a.m. moments.
I should go home. I should run out the back
fucking door, but then I won't get to see the
ceiling beams and cinders come down on all of us-
I'd miss the ash swallowing up skin and hair laced with
touched-up mirror lipstick and
momentary love.

It'll be closed soon,
quiet soon.
My world will soon be dust

if I just wait.

Compromises

I hate sleep
I tell God he owes me the 1/3 of my life
stolen by slumber.
I can't get shit done
drifting toward what dreams may come.

riding a night wind
through my witching hour
God speaks:

*bitch if you didn't pass out some of the time, you'd be
    fuckin dead*

Worked

I realize that Frost
is fine and that one
shouldn't be a Kant,
but I prefer *Carmelita*
to getting blood on the tracks.

A cigarette and a love
poem is cliche, but half
an Ambien and a bottle of
whiskey washed down
with year-old hash
oil from a bong will write
three verses for you.

A great poet shoved her head
in an oven.

I just don't want to listen to the gas.

Pen Name

I wrote erotica for a summer
to tow my mind out of a ditch muddied with the
poetry of pain. Sex sells better, finely dressed or
window-shopped and cheap.
I skip ads on television, but the ones I catch
are fast and dirty
loud and flashy.
-from car parts to cruises,
all a million different ways to say every day
would be better with a boner-
or whatever god damn car or pill
that can make you hard,
even though all that chasing just makes a man soft.
One nation under God, smut sells easy-
plenty of followers on their knees.

*Under the table, her hand closed around his. The tip of her finger
circled his knuckle in suggestive strokes. She could hear the breath
catch in his throat. She slid an outstretched finger back and forth
over the stem of the wine glass, waiting for him to finally exhale -
her foot clutched up under his calf through the thin strap of her
sandal -*

Work from home

There is nothing to do
I am too tired to move
But my skin is screaming,
get up
get up and move
you sack of shit!
For god's sake,
smash the ticking clock
twist its arms
speed them up
slow them down
or just rip them off.

Something.
Do something

I drink coffee for two hours
wasting
wasting away
a life so long
so frustratingly out of reach
the clock's arms are wrapped up in paychecks
a schedule nice and neat.

Matthew 19:24

Biden bends over for Bezos,
whose bitch ass should have blown
up in space if there was a God.
Leaving us to cough up our lungs
and our futures while lying
through our teeth to children
that are going to see a worse
world than we got.
An aforementioned,
pre-destined boomer promise,
dick-stamped by Reagan and a
million other Elephants and
Donkey's all forming a line
to suck big ol' money's cock-
Little Ramses, plasterboard monuments
of the men that feed on us all.
The people crushed
in Flint and Charlottesville
under the boot of so many
god damn Nazis
that we have
to treat them like a voting block
now. Eye of a fucking
needle, indeed.

Good one Jesus.

Last week some lady ran out in front of my car

to climb into my soul and die there.
Begging for the steel cage keeping us six feet apart
to ferry her into six pieces and seven hells.
OUT OF THE ROAD YOU CRAZY BITCH!
is a terrible thing to yell at a suicidal person,
but I am already carrying too much
to keep her corpse in front of my eyelids.

Baptism - God is a man's black heart

Torture   slows
      down
time
waterboarding only lasts for 13 seconds

Love makes life a twinkling, while
pain grants eternal life.
Pain is a time machine,
pain is etched on skin, it scars
pain is
a gift
the gift of
god
the God of the Christians
the God of death. God,
      Oh God, oh God oh
            God is killing
doctors in Oklahoma and Texas ,
shooting up schools in Colorado,
lovers in Wyoming.
Bow your head.
Clasp your fingers
when the beast passes. Red and yellow,
black and white, we
the meat
in his sight.

Yahweh - Allah - King of Kings
he wants more wants more wants more.

Apathetic Lead

There was a shooting at the high school
near our home and one block over,
over god or god knows what. The panic. The panic.
People fucking shoot people
I hear none of it I see
none of it. I don't even put
down my coffee, skim the news,
or gawk out the window. I take out
the dog. I put out the trash.
When the sirens pass the window
I don't even raise my head.

Allfather

Huginn and Muninn are in my yard picking through mud.
Hoisting worms in the air, little snips of their beaks
scissor them in half

A squirrel scratches his head reading a
treasure map for gems he left at X.

Raindrops make long journeys across eaves and branches
before diving into the driveway collective

I, hungover, greet them from my vinyl throne on the porch.
Smoking the grass. Hair of the dog. Before I join them
in the dirt.

Haunted

Ghosts are at my door again,
scratching with chipped fingernails
down wood and peeling paint. I peek
through fingers threaded over my face.
Behind me in the mirror. They twist
at the doorknobs to the basement's black pit-
pulling cobwebs into veils. Lurking. Crawling
across the faces of old photos I keep in a duffle bag
at the bottom of a closet.
Wearing Mickey Mouse ears and an old mustache,
they are dead, dead, dead.
Faded Kodak. Bottomless wells
of pallor mortis, crying down the hallway
and creaking up the stairs of my thoughts
like a shadow across the moon.
They can float right through
the oaken studs and plaster,
but beg me to let them in.

Halloween Dad

I told them for weeks the trick or treaters
would come and line the blocks.
We filled bowl after bowl and sat
on the porch in costumes costing more than
any of us would make the next month.
No one came. We danced on the porch and
laughed and walked downtown.
I couldn't help thinking
this was another promise I had failed to keep.

Penciled

in
case I change my mind
in the margins
away from   what matters
feinting with rubber
applied with aggression
nothing more human than engineering
a do over.

ink only scratches at ~~what~~
~~it doesn't like;~~
the voyeur still
traces the deep grooves
of soft paper with
trembling fingertips,
feeling through black blinds to see
what's underneath.

Moonlit Path

I walk a moonlit path,
starving myself of sleep
and sanity - sometimes.
A symphony of night calls me,
The last act for the
evening - a cricket's encore
is a lullaby for lovers,
dancing down the bricks
of a river park.

Quiet.

I watch each
porch go dark,
and wonder what it's like
in there - a room with
Christmas dinners and
stupid sweaters.
"Where are you?"
When I'm running late-

Crash.

A raccoon tips over a
trashcan with his wife
and kids.

I walk a moonlit path, alone,
but at the very last notes
the whole world sings for me.

Kiss

Dry leaves slide
across concrete.
They sound like Pop Rocks,
or a million tiny heels scurrying
after a bus.
On a windy day,
the shuffle is
hushed and crackling,
urgent- the way two bodies
start to take in each other's air.

When I say I love you

When I say I love you
I hate the sound love makes
when it drifts from lips.
I say no hands are like your hands;
my skin has never been so safe.
Fingertips ignite one nerve at a time
needling a record of me   pausing
in the tangles of my chest, I catch
your breath in the pocket of my collarbone
and weep. Born of a midnight fear,
when I say I love you,
I hope I will tomorrow.

Vesper

I was born into bondage
to a God I never met.
I heard the call of the moon, bright stars,
and set my path to nowhere. To know and care,
for a place with no crosses or death, just one,
single
apple.
Or maybe a pear.
A place where my children sit on blankets and
count cloud beasts in the air.
Where they live with and without fear and
have-   choice.
Just choice and dreams.
No expectations or eternity to bear.
Just open eyes
to see. Space to be,
and breathe.

Maybe they will worship a tree, maybe
there will be nothing to believe.

That would be ok
with me.

Forty

for Jennifer

It's 2022,
and age forty looms.
Father twice, third time
soon.
I settled before; now
settled down.
    alright,
I'll never settle down,
but I am back down
from the moon-
a cold mistress,
lightless, lifeless,
and lonely cocoon.
Rocket Man crash
landing in the arms
of my lover,
the one I gave room.
To make space,
I had to let go
of *you.*
She sits with me
as I write this,
too. A life in
bloom.
Her belly full of
rose petals,
first notes of a song;
to carry,
carry on
our shared tune.

Preacher

I'm just a preacher
I never wanted it, or
wanted to be
anything
but me
to let alone and be left alone.
There are more reasons
than I can count
why
I shouldn't be
this,
here,

three hours deep
in a lecture on vowels
power points on communication
pushing public speaking
the god damn projector, broken-
shit roof is leaking,
email maintenance.

Keep on keeping. Keep on
keeping on.
Can I correct them
without making them feel
wrong?

I was born with a mouthful of words
that spilled out on a hospital floor.

Nonstop flustered barrage from the
moment they cut the ripcord.
The first one, not momma or dadda,
but car. I'm still driving
my childhood away to Disneyland
or Tomorrowland or somewhere
it can land without crushing us both.
Jesus, thanks for the cross and shit,
but no need to pay my bill.
My sins are on a tab I'm running still.
I'm just a preacher.

Behind podiums and desks,
books and students, deadlines
and this need to talk, talk, talk-
tired talk
now talk
the rock I build on,
my holy ground,
a flock of students
a god of knowledge
and thought.

Primary Target

When the door slams,
When the door slams shut.
When the door slams shut we
Hide.
When the door slams shut we
Chuckle.   *nervous*
When the door slams shut we give
Sighs.   *relief*
We the door slams shut we give
Thanks.

It wasn't a bullet,
          we're all still alive.

Decent

Decent people, plenty of decent people pay their bills on time and don't owe a god damn dime to anyone - anyone but god. Sparing and stopping change falling downward toward the unavoidable debt to time. Decent people pray, decent people pet their dog and don't leave their trash bin at the curb a second past the trash truck's whine. Decent people bow their head. Decent people get in line. Decent people love to buid a big ol' pyre and burn, burn anyone not kneeling in radiant *white* light.

Rob Yates is an artist living in Hutchinson, KS working within a variety of mediums. Rob toured as a punk musician with The Klyk through the late nineties and early 2000s. He has produced and directed two independent films, recorded two albums, and published various short stories and poetry. Most recently, he exhibitioned a series of paintings and continued his twentieth year of acting in and writing/ directing local theatre productions. He is a father to three daughters and one Husky named Yoshi. Outside of creative pursuits, he travels the Rockies and makes a mean curry.

This project was made possible, in part, by generous support from the Osage Arts Community.

Osage Arts Community provides temporary time, space and support for the creation of new artistic works in a retreat format, serving creative people of all kinds — visual artists, composers, poets, fiction and nonfiction writers. Located on a 152-acre farm in an isolated rural mountainside setting in Central Missouri and bordered by ¾ of a mile of the Gasconade River, OAC provides residencies to those working alone, as well as welcoming collaborative teams, offering living space and workspace in a country environment to emerging and mid-career artists. For more information, visit us at www.osageac.org

Osage Arts Community